Angel At McDonald's

Advent Drama For Youth

Linda M. Goens

CSS Publishing Company, Inc., Lima, Ohio

ANGEL AT McDONALD'S

For more information about CSS Publishing Company resources, visit our website at
www.csspub.com.

ISBN 978-0-7880-7841-1   PRINTED IN U.S.A.

To the youth of
Church of the Saviour,
in Indianapolis, Indiana,
whose energy and goodness
ever inspire me.

Angel At McDonald's

Advent Drama For Youth

Notes

Sets can be elaborate, but the play is designed so that only signs are needed to establish the activity center and McDonald's. A manger scene or cross or just a lone manger with doll will indicate the sanctuary.

The author's youth group performed this play as Readers' Theatre, though they used quite a bit of action and props, including the knife, the cloth, and the manger. Stage directions were read by a narrator.

Characters

Lina — a teenage female, the sweet, shy type

Casey — a teenage female, talkative, sarcastic sometimes, aggressive appearance

Angel — male or female with a sense of humor, teenage or adult

Jerome — male gang leader, gruff, even fierce

Patricia — Jerome's sister, also tough, but approachable

Frankie — male or female, friend and sidekick of Jerome

Non-speaking roles — additional youth and one child

Setting

An urban youth center

An outdoor trash bin at McDonald's

A church sanctuary

Suggested Props

Scenes 1 and 4

A sign proclaiming "Downing Square Youth Activity Center"

Table with punch bowl, cups, and plate with cookies

Any Christmas decorations

Gift bags with toys

A knife for Jerome

Scenes 2 and 3
A sign with "McDonald's — Trash Bin, Do Not Park" or a large
  container with "McDonald's Trash" printed on side
A large plastic trash bag
A beautiful piece of fabric, such as gold lame

Scene 5
A cross and/or a manger scene

Scene 1

(A sign declares the place as Downing Square Youth Activity Center. There are plates of goodies and a bowl of punch on a nearby table. LINA and CASEY, accompanied by other youth, are decorating for Christmas.)

Lina: I thought we were decorating *with* the kids from the youth center, not *for* them.

Casey: No amount of decorating is going to change this dump.

Lina: Maybe they think the same thing and that's why they didn't come.

Casey: It's our pastor who gets us into this stuff. Why can't he be like the last one and just preach at us?

Lina: Because he cares about the underprivileged. Hand me the tape, will you?

Casey: *(Looks around)* I don't see him here. Do you see him here caring about the underprivileged? For that matter, where are the underprivileged?

Lina: From the looks of this neighborhood, I'm not so sure I want anybody here but us.

Casey: You have nothing to fear but fear itself. Besides, there's a security guard around here somewhere and two adult leaders, also somewhere.

Lina: Well, the place makes me nervous. Let's sing Christmas carols. Maybe that will help.

(CASEY begins singing "Frosty The Snowman" and is joined by a few others.)

Lina: That is not a Christmas carol.

(*CASEY begins singing "Hark, The Herald Angels Sing." LINA joins in. Enter JEROME, PATRICIA, and FRANKIE with a few others. They are fierce-looking and angry. The girls slowly quit singing.*)

Casey: (*Bravely*) Hi.

(*JEROME, PATRICIA and FRANKIE walk among the decorations, clearly disgusted with what they see.*)

Casey: My name is Casey. This is Lina. We're from ...

Frankie: We don't care where you're from.

(*The three continue their silent inspection.*)

Lina: (*With false cheer*) Are you going to help decorate?

Patricia: (*To FRANKIE*) So! That's what all this trash is supposed to be, decoration!

Frankie: (*In CASEY's face*) Nice try, but give it up!

Lina: Help yourself to the food. (*Pauses*) Please, it's for everybody.

Jerome: (*Sarcastically*) Even us.

Frankie: Oh, of course it's for us. They came to feed the poor. And we, in case you didn't know, are the poor.

Casey: No. It's for everybody. Us, too. That is, I ...

Jerome: (*In CASEY's face*) I've got an idea. Why don't you go home?

Casey: Where are the little kids? The cookies and punch are for the little kids.

Patricia: We don't want your cookies and your punch.

Frankie: Or your stupid decorations.

Casey: Then why did you come in?

Lina: Casey, be quiet!

Jerome: That's right, Casey, be quiet! As you leave, be very quiet and maybe you won't get hurt.

Casey: You're the reason the little ones didn't come, aren't you? I'll bet they wanted to come, and you kept them out.

Lina: (*To CASEY*) Casey, shut up!

Patricia: We don't want our kids around you. So, go!

Lina: Come on, Casey.

Casey: I don't think this is right. The little kids ought to be allowed to ...

Frankie: Don't you get it? We don't want you here. You do what the little wimp says. Go home to your big fancy house and count the big fat presents under your big fat tree.

Lina: We brought presents for the little kids. Toys. We were going to give them out after ...

Patricia: You are a fool. You come in here once a year, feed our kids a few cookies, hand them some stupid toy that breaks in a week, and go back to the suburbs feeling like a saint. Well, this year, you ain't feeling like no saint at my expense. Get out of here. (*Grabs bags of toys as LINA and CASEY head for the door*) And take these toys with you.

(*LINA and CASEY exit with toys.*)

9

Jerome: (*Yells*) This is not a safe neighborhood. I suggest you don't come back.

(*A small child comes in. She takes an eager step toward the punch and cookies. PATRICIA takes the child's hand and walks with her toward the punch. FRANKIE grabs the child's hand and, with an angry look at PATRICIA, leads the child out of the center into the dark, cold night.*)

Scene 2

(*It is Christmas Eve, early afternoon, at McDonald's. LINA has been working since early morning. After taking out a bag of trash, she will be ready to go home. The trash bin is nearly full, and LINA has to shove things out of the way to make room for the bag. It is for this reason she doesn't immediately see the ANGEL who approaches.*)

Angel: Lina.

Lina: Who is it? (*Pauses*) What? What are you?

Angel: Don't be afraid.

Lina: (*Stammers*) You're ... you're an ... an angel.

Angel: That's right. An angel from the Lord. And I've been sent to give you a message.

Lina: Oh, no. No, not me. Please, not me. I'm not the one you want.

Angel: You don't even know what I'm going to say. Why are you saying no?

Lina: Because every time an angel shows up in the Bible, someone ends up doing something really bizarre.

Angel: I never looked at it quite like that.

Lina: So, I can just go back inside, right? And you'll find someone else.

Angel: I think you should hear the message. Then decide.

Lina: (*Resignedly*) I don't have a choice, do I?

Angel: Actually, no.

Lina: Okay. (*Pauses*) I'm ready. Tell me.

Angel: You have been chosen to deliver the Good News to the young people of Downing Square, specifically to their leader, Jerome Hadley.

Lina: The good news? What good news?

Angel: Come on, now, Lina. I assume our Lord selected you at least in part for some degree of intelligence.

Lina: You mean, about Jesus? About his coming to save the world from sin? And how he loves everyone?

Angel: That's the one.

Lina: (*Appalled*) You want me to go to Downing Square and tell that ... that Jerome about Jesus? Me?

Angel: Yes, you.

Lina: Are you for real?

Angel: You know that I am.

Lina: And you came from the Lord?

Angel: You know that I did.

Lina: So this isn't your idea; it's God's?

Angel: Yes.

Lina: Why me?

Angel: I think this is the place where you are supposed to say, "Let it be according to Thy will."

Lina: You don't want me for this mission. I won't get past the first sentence. One of them called me a wimp, and it's true. I'm scared to death of those people. I can't do it.

Angel: It's not my idea, remember?

Lina: You need someone strong and brave. I mean, I'm not even brave enough to talk to my speech class without my legs shaking so badly I can hardly stand up. Even if Jerome lets me talk, which he won't, I couldn't say a word, I'd be so scared.

Angel: No sense arguing with me. I'm just the messenger.

Lina: What you need is a guy, better yet, a big guy, a really big, powerful-looking guy. Most of those kids at the center are (*Hesitates*) well, street-wise. You know? They're tough. They don't want to hear some wimpy white girl from the suburbs preach about Jesus.

Angel: So, you want me to tell the Lord you said, "No." Would that be "No, thanks" or just plain "No"?

Lina: The Lord. I ... I guess I don't want to tell the Lord, "No," do I?

Angel: It's your choice. You don't have to do it.

Lina: How about this? How about you send my friend, Casey. She stood right up to them. You should have heard her ... (*Pauses*) I guess you probably did hear her. Anyway, nobody can talk as well as Casey. She got a standing ovation for her speech on freedom at the last assembly, and she isn't scared of anything. I mean, nothing.

Angel: She isn't, huh?

Lina: So, you want me to go get her?

Angel: Sure, you can go get her.

Lina: Great! This is the best thing. I'll go with her, if you want.

Angel: Lina.

Lina: This is the best way to handle it.

Angel: Lina.

Lina: She can do the talking ...

Angel: Lina.

Lina: ... and I'll be sort of a support person.

Angel: Lina.

Lina: Yes, that's it, a support person. I'm good at that.

Angel: Lina! All I said was you can go get her.

Lina: Oh, okay, then. I'll be right back.

Angel: (*Stops her*) Tonight will be fine. Now, then, I have something to give you.

Lina: What? (*ANGEL pulls out gold cloth*) Wow! That's beautiful.

Angel: You are to give this cloth to Jerome with the following instructions: He is to lay it in the manger at church on Christmas Eve as evidence of his belief that Jesus was sent to save everybody, including him.

Lina: What if he won't take it? What if he tears it up?

Angel: The cloth is sacred. It must not be damaged or lost.

Lina: I don't see how you can expect me to do this! I'm not the right person, I tell you.

Angel: Jerome has to take the cloth of his own free will, but once it is in his possession, it is up to him what happens to it.

Lina: But you said it was sacred. How come it doesn't matter what he does with it?

Angel: I didn't say that. I said it's up to Jerome what happens to it. It's your job to make sure he understands, and once he does, you are through.

Lina: Do you know what kind of guy we're dealing with here?

Angel: Yes.

Lina: I'm scared.

Angel: God would not send you into the lions' den without his protection. Do you believe that?

Lina: Yes (*Pauses*) But you did say I can take Casey? (*ANGEL is leaving*) Where are you going? (*ANGEL leaves*) Wait a minute. (*To herself, as she leaves*) Casey, you've got to help me.

Scene 3

(It is early evening at McDonald's.)

Casey: So, where is this — ah — Angel?

Lina: I didn't say he would be here waiting for us. Angels don't wait for us; we wait for angels. That's how it works.

Casey: Right. *(They sit and wait)* Now, tell me again why an angel wants to meet me at a McDonald's trash bin.

Lina: He wants to ask you something, but I don't know why here. I don't know why he met me here. It's sure to be private, maybe that's why. *(They wait some more)*

Casey: It's Christmas Eve. It's dark. It's almost time for church, and I'm sitting by a trash bin waiting for an angel. This is crazy. *(Starts out)* I'm going home.

Lina: No! Please. Casey, you're my best friend. Please don't leave. You have to help me. Please!

Casey: Help you what? What is going on?

Lina: You do believe me about the angel, don't you? *(CASEY doesn't answer)* Case? You don't believe me.

Casey: What do you expect? Lina! An angel? Here?

Lina: It's true. I spoke with an angel right here.

Casey: Then where is your angel?

Lina: I don't know. *(Pauses)* Now that I think of it, he didn't actually say he would talk to you. He agreed that you could help me, that's all.

15

Casey: Help you what?

Lina: He gave me a message. (*Hesitates*) I am to go to Downing Square to tell Jerome about Jesus.

Casey: (*Incredulously*) Excuse me?

Lina: I'm supposed to tell him — well, all of them, really — that Jesus was born to save people from their sins, that he will always love them.

Casey: You want me to help you tell a gang leader that Jesus will save him from his sins.

Lina: Actually, I was rather hoping you would do it.

Casey: An angel gave you this message. From God, I presume.

Lina: Yes.

Casey: I'm going home. (*Starts to leave again*)

Lina: I'll have to go alone then.

Casey: No, you are not going to Downing Square alone.

Lina: I have to.

Casey: You mean it? You are really going to do this?

Lina: It's a request, Casey. From God. Would you say, "No," to God?

Casey: I guess I'd better not even say, "No," to you.

Lina: Then you will go?

Casey: Yes. Can we take Mr. Cartwright or the pastor?

Lina: Nobody else. I had a hard enough time getting you in on this mission.

Casey: Gee, thanks.

Lina: The angel gave me this. (*Removes cloth and hands it to CASEY*) It's a sacred cloth. I think there must be a lot of gold in it.

Casey: I've never seen anything so beautiful. It feels like a cloud. Why on earth didn't you show me this in the first place?

Lina: I wanted you to believe me, I guess. Without proof. Anyway, I could have gotten the cloth at a fabric store.

Casey: Not one like this, you couldn't.

Lina: We're supposed to give this to Jerome, and he, in turn, is supposed to lay it in the manger at church. The angel told me the cloth must not be lost or damaged.

Casey: I don't think I would give it to Jerome then.

Lina: Whether he does or doesn't accept the cloth and what he does with it afterward is his responsibility. All we have to do is offer it and have faith that God will do the rest.

Casey: Okay, but I don't think we should start right out telling this guy his sins will be forgiven. Let's not refer to sins at all. We can talk about love. No one takes offense at love, but sin — Jerome isn't going to like being accused of sin.

Lina: (*Stops and looks at her friend*) Only you would change a message from God to one you like better.

Casey: Are you kidding? Have you ever been to a Bible study?

17

Lina: It's getting late, Casey. We've got to go.

Casey: (*They start out but CASEY stops suddenly*) I don't think I can do this.

Lina: Why?

Casey: Why? You're taking me to the ghetto at night to tell a gang leader about Jesus. I'm scared to death, that's why.

Lina: You weren't scared at the Christmas party. I was amazed at the way you talked right back to them, like they didn't bother you one little bit. I was so scared I couldn't talk at all.

Casey: I thought you knew me better than that. When I don't know how to handle a situation, I talk fast and I talk big. It keeps me from fainting or crying.

Lina: God wouldn't send us into a lions' den without protection. That's what the angel said.

Casey: And you believe it?

Lina: Yes, I guess I do.

Casey: All right then, let's go face the lions.

Scene 4

(*Later that evening, JEROME enters a dark, empty activity center. He is followed by PATRICIA and FRANKIE. He seems to be looking for something or someone.*)

Frankie: What are we doing here? (*No answer*) Jerome? What are we doing here?

Patricia: Jerome! It's Christmas Eve.

18

Jerome: So?

Patricia: So, what are we doing at the activity center on Christmas Eve?

Jerome: I got a feeling ...

Patricia: You got a feeling. (*To FRANKIE*) He's got a feeling.

Frankie: A feeling about what?

Jerome: Something told me to be here, all right. Now shut up about it.

Frankie: (*After a pause*) This is stupid.

Patricia: (*After another pause*) It is stupid! Jerome?

Jerome: You don't want to be here, go home.

(*When LINA and CASEY suddenly walk in the door, JEROME is startled. When he pulls a knife, the girls stop, frozen.*)

Jerome: What are you doing here?

Lina: We came to see you (*Pauses*) and your ... ah ... friends.

Jerome: (*Checks behind them*) Who'd you bring with you?

Lina: We came alone.

Frankie: They're dumber than I thought.

Patricia: You came alone to see us on Christmas Eve.

Jerome: (*To PATRICIA*) What's with you and this Christmas Eve stuff? Shut up about it. (*To LINA and CASEY*) What do you want?

19

Lina: We came to deliver a message.

Jerome: (*Highly suspicious*) From who?

Lina: An angel. Well, actually from God, but the angel was the one who talked to me, directly.

Jerome: Girl, you're crazy.

Lina: I know it's hard to believe.

Jerome: You're right, and I don't believe it. Get out of here. I told you before to never come back. Now, move! (*Threatens them with the knife*)

Patricia: I think you should hear the message.

Jerome: Because it's Christmas Eve, right?

Patricia: They came here — alone. Can't you see how scared they are?

Frankie: They ought to be scared.

Patricia: Would they be here if there wasn't a good reason? Listen to the message. What can it hurt?

Jerome: All right. Deliver your message and get out!

(*LINA and CASEY try to push each other forward.*)

Jerome: Come on. Come on. Let's get on with it.

Lina: God wants you to know that Jesus came to ...

Casey: Love us. (*JEROME stares at them*) All of us, including you.

Lina: And to deliver us ...

Casey: Don't tell him that.

Lina: I have to. Jesus came to love us and to deliver us from our sins.

Jerome: That so? Okay. Cool. (*Pauses for a sudden burst of real anger*) Get out of here! (*Furiously*) Now!

Patricia: Jerome, stop it.

Frankie: Don't stop him! They need to learn a lesson.

Patricia: They brought a message from God!

Frankie: (*Disgustedly*) God.

Jerome: I'm going to warn you one more time.

Patricia: No, Jerome. Let them stay. You said earlier, something told you to be here. Well, it was probably a nudge from God. I've heard of that. God was speaking to you and ...

Jerome: Why don't you go with them?

Lina: We aren't going anywhere.

Casey: Lina, come on!

Lina: (*To CASEY*) The cloth. I have to give him the cloth.

Casey: Are you crazy? He's not going to take that cloth.

Jerome: You are asking for it, Girl.

Lina: You haven't heard the whole message. I can't go until I finish. (*Pulls out cloth and shows it to him*) This is a sacred gold cloth. It must not be damaged or lost, and I am to give it to ...

Casey: ... anyone here.

Lina: Casey, that's not what the angel said. I was told to ...

Casey: (*To LINA*) You said you wanted my help. If you keep quiet, you'll get it. (*To PATRICIA, FRANKIE, and JEROME*) This sacred cloth signifies that the holder believes in Jesus. That Jesus was sent by God to love us, to take away our sins, and to make us like new people. Anyone who holds this cloth will not only demonstrate great courage but possess courage in all situations forever.

Lina: Casey! That's not ...

Casey: The cloth must be placed in the manger at church as a gift to Jesus, acknowledging his birth and his love. Anyone placing the gift of this sacred cloth will show great courage. Isn't that right, Lina?

Lina: Well, yes, I guess so.

Jerome: (*Eyes the cloth*) You're both nuts. (*The others get closer to look at the cloth*)

Patricia: It's beautiful!

Casey: Yes, it is.

Patricia: Look, Frankie.

Frankie: Stay away from me with that thing.

Patricia: (*To CASEY*) An angel gave you this?

Casey: Not me. Her. (*Points to LINA*)

Patricia: Then the cloth is what gave her the courage to come here.

Casey: Well, I don't know. I suppose.

Frankie: Are you believing this stuff?

Patricia: They're here, aren't they?

Frankie: They're stupid, okay? Stupid. And so are you if you believe them.

Lina: It's a funny thing. You need courage to take the cloth in the first place, but once you have it, you know God is with you and you get braver and braver.

(*PATRICIA reaches out for the cloth.*)

Jerome: Give me that thing! (*Snatches the cloth and carries it around draped over his knife*)

Patricia: Don't tear it!

Casey: Don't!

Lina: (*To CASEY*) Remember, Case, once he takes the cloth, it's up to him what he does with it.

Patricia: You said it can't be damaged. I heard you. Jerome, please, be careful.

Lina: The angel said to bring the cloth to church and place it in the manger.

Jerome: Why should I?

Casey: To show you believe Jesus really came to save you.

Frankie: (*Disgustedly*) Oh, please!

Jerome: Maybe I don't believe. Maybe I believe this is one heck of an expensive piece of material that could bring me a whole lot of money. Maybe I'll just tuck this rag in my back pocket or tie it over my head. Maybe I'll just use it to shine my shoes.

Casey: You gotta play the role, don't you? That's sacred, from God. And you dare to talk about shining your shoes with it. Give it here. Give it back.

Lina: (*Stops her*) Casey, no.

Frankie: Leave her alone. I'd like to see her take that thing from Jerome.

Lina: Casey, what he does with the cloth is his responsibility now. You know that. We're through here. Come on. Let's go.

(*LINA and CASEY exit while the others stay put and watch in silence.*)

Frankie: An angel. Oh, sure. It must have been a dare.

Scene 5
(*It is after services on Christmas Eve, and there is no one around. PATRICIA enters the sanctuary and falls to her knees at the manger scene.*)

Patricia: (*Prays*) Oh, God, what am I doing? Why am I here? (*Pauses*) I'm so afraid.

(*The ANGEL appears unseen, or this could be a recorded voice.*)

Angel: Do not be afraid. I bring you good news of great joy. The Savior has been born to you on this night. He is with you now and will never leave you. His love is yours and his courage and his redemption. Though this world is full of pain and suffering, there will never again be anything you cannot handle. For Christ is with you. Glory to God in the highest. (*Exits*)

(*Enter CASEY and LINA, talking.*)

Lina: We have to quit worrying about Jerome. He is in God's hands.

Casey: I know, but ... look, it's Patricia!

Lina: I can't believe it.

Patricia: (*Jumps to her feet*) I'm sorry. I was just, that is, I mean, I didn't think anyone would still be here.

Casey: We're supposed to take down the manger display, but we were waiting ... hoping that ...

Patricia: You hoped Jerome would come. Well, he won't.

Lina: You came. I'm glad you came.

Patricia: So am I. It's true about the angel. He spoke to me. I didn't exactly see him, but he was here.

Casey: You don't have to see things to believe they exist. I guess I've learned that this Christmas. Patricia, I have an idea. Remember the bags of toys we brought to the center last week and Jerome made us take them home?

Patricia: I made you take them home.

Lina: We didn't take them home. The toys are here, at the church.

Casey: Would you take them with you now? You could distribute them in your family or neighborhood.

Patricia: Why don't we all give them out? We can leave toys on front porches up and down the street. They'd be there tomorrow when the kids wake up. (*Hesitates*) Unless you don't feel it's safe.

Lina: You just talked to an angel. What do you think?

Patricia: Let's go.

Casey: What about the manger scene? We promised to put everything away.

Lina: No, I don't think we had better do it right now. Next week will be soon enough.

(*The girls exit. JEROME enters the sanctuary when he's sure no one is there. He tosses the cloth on the manger.*)

Jerome: I did what you told me to do, but don't expect me to kneel or nothin'. (*Stares at the doll in the manger angrily*) This world is a mess. You know that? (*FRANKIE enters, unseen by JEROME*) My world is a mess. (*Pauses*) They say you bring peace and love. I don't see it. I see fighting and hate. You have to fight, you know, to keep what's yours. To keep your self-respect.

Frankie: I can't believe you are talking to a doll.

Jerome: You could get hurt messing around places you aren't supposed to be.

Frankie: I can't believe it. You're taking those snotty rich girls seriously? You believe they talked to an angel?

Jerome: It ain't none of your business what I believe. Get lost.

Frankie: I don't have no respect for a dude that talks to no doll.

Jerome: I can get along without your respect.

Frankie: (*Angrily*) There ain't no such thing as angels!

Jerome: How do you know?

Frankie: You ever seen one? While you was sober, that is?

Jerome: (*Considers*) Maybe.

Frankie: Maybe? Maybe? Man, what's wrong with you?

Jerome: (*Takes the cloth from the manger*) Take the cloth, Frankie.

Frankie: I ain't touching that thing.

Jerome: Come on, take it. Just hold it a minute. (*Pauses*) You chicken?

Frankie: I don't believe in no angels. And no God either. (*Pauses*) You're lost, brother. You're lost! (*FRANKIE exits as if scared*)

Jerome: (*Starts after FRANKIE, pleading*) Frankie! Frank ... Man, you're the one that's lost. (*Wanders back to manger, considering, as he examines the cloth, caresses it. Looks at the manger or cross or some other symbol of Christ. He pauses*) Do I have this right? I give you this piece of cloth; you give me love and courage. And you forgive my sins, too. It's a pretty good deal, I guess. Considering the cloth wasn't mine in the first place. (*Kneels at the manger*) Okay, man, here I am.

The End

www.ingramcontent.com/pod-product-compliance
Lightning Source LLC
Chambersburg PA
CBHW071808020426
42331CB00008B/2444